AF439766

Shattered Pieces Mended with Gold

Robin Ricci

Table of Contents

Introduction

When I was younger, I couldn't fathom the life I am leading now. I had no idea—no concept of the option—that I would have two beautiful children that fill my life with unconditional love. I wasn't even aware of how special love really is. The possibility of having a man in my life accept me, love me, bolster me and help me and take care of me wasn't even in the stratosphere. I didn't even know to have the hope for building a life that was nothing like the trauma I had faced. I learned so many valuable lessons while moving through all of this. Not all men are abusive. Not all men will hurt you. And unconditional love is real. I know, because now, that's my reality.

My earliest memory is of getting my picture taken. I remember holding a Christmas present and having the worst bowl haircut of my life. It was somewhere between three and five years old. That haircut stuck with me through most of my life up until I was in high school. That's just one example of the extreme control, my father had over me. He went to every single haircut I had and told them exactly how I had to have my hair. He also went to Walmart and made me get my clothes from the boy section. He made me wear them to school. This was my entire elementary school time. He controlled me on an extreme level.

We moved houses more times than I can even remember, and I think it was just because he was so afraid of getting caught. I remember him fighting with my mom a lot. I remember a bookcase that was in front of a glass wall and he got so mad one time that he hit the bookcase against that glass wall and it shattered all over the living room carpet. That made him so mad, that he ended up pushing the bookcase onto me. It hurt really badly, but luckily I was small enough that it didn't actually break anything. I remember just lying there with this immense bookcase on top of me and then him scrambling to pretend like it was an accident when it really wasn't. I remember very vividly sleeping in bed with my blanket, my favorite blanket in the whole world—I was probably five or six—him storming in my room in the middle of night and just ripping that blanket up into shreds. It just killed me that he could even do that.

It makes me wonder because it's there had been multiple nights that he just decided to wake up at three in the morning or four in the morning and destroy something that I loved. When I was older and was into makeup, because I had acne and he made fun of me, I wanted to cover it up. He went into the bathroom and started just smashing my makeup and broke my straightener in half and threw it all down the toilet. When I asked why he did that, he had no answer. I remember him trying to tell me that I had done something wrong, but I had been just lying in bed, not doing anything.

It didn't stop there.

Trapped

While those memories are very clear to me, what I'll share next isn't as clear. Although, in saying that, if it didn't happen how I remember, then I don't see why he would have offered me money in return for my silence. I remember walking past my sister and brother's room around 15 or 16 years old, and crawling into my father's bed and giving him a blow job. He didn't finish, but I remember feeling gross and guilty so I stopped. He tried to tell me it was fine, it wasn't his fault because I wanted it. It couldn't be further from the truth. I didn't want anything to do with it. It's not as clear as some other memories. I think it's fuzzy because I just disassociated during all of that. This also wouldn't be the last of it.

I remember just lying there and praying to God that I would find someone to come and rescue me from the abuse. He controlled me so much. I couldn't have friends, I couldn't go anywhere after school. I was in choir because I loved to sing, but he wouldn't let me do any of the performances or let me stay after school for anything. I had volleyball and I had to quit because the games were after school. He wouldn't let me shower on the weekends because then I would look somewhat pretty and would possibly get the attention of boys and he wanted me to feel like the worst possible shit about myself. At any given moment, if I looked beautiful, he would pinch my nipples in public or comment about them in public. He would say I have 'back acne' in public. Anything he could to destroy my confidence. He did that for many many many years and still continues to do it because I'm allowing it to affect me still.

Another time, my father and I were playing ball with a somewhat bigger than normal bouncy ball and we were throwing it, and I somehow hit him on the temple. He got so mad at me, he whipped the ball at me as hard as he could and hit me in the vagina. It hit so hard it cut my skin. I was crying at the top of the stairs. I was only ten or eleven.

I felt trapped. I identified with Rapunzel because she was locked in a tower by someone who supposedly loved her. Her mother. Later we find out it's not her mother. That's really similar to my life. Looking at pictures of my mom, I look nothing like her. Looking at pictures of my dad, I look nothing like him. But looking at pictures of my mom's sister and I look a hell of a lot like her for some reason. Rapunzel eventually decides to leave her tower, which I did too at 18 years old. I went to the safest place I knew on earth. Disney World. I was accepted for an internship with the Walt Disney Company and it was the biggest opportunity I had ever had. I remember getting ready by restricting food. I only ate 300 calories a day for almost 3 months. I passed out at the gym because I wasn't eating enough and I snapped out of it after losing 50 pounds. The control I found with restricting food was so enticing that I still struggle with the thought.

No Magical Kingdom

I was wrong about Walt Disney World. It wasn't the safest place on earth. Nowhere was because I would find love in the wrong people. I ended up in abusive relationships because it was what I was used to and all I thought I deserved. He let me go. I think he thought I was safe there, or that I would get scared and come back home. I remember crying on the plane when I left. He hugged me and was crying and kept telling me he loved me. That made it worse because he had never said that before. I was second-guessing myself on the plane and crying because I had no one. I was doing this alone. All on my own. But I said, you know what? I'm going to fucking do it!

The hardest part about that was leaving behind my siblings. I thought I was protecting them. Especially my brother. I literally raised that kid. I was ten years old when he was born. I remember lying in bed downstairs in the basement with him as a newborn and I would pray over him and I would make sure he was okay. He was my best friend. The hardest part of leaving was feeling like I abandoned him. I didn't want him to feel like I didn't care about him. Lord knows what my father told him.

Essentially, after three months of me being gone, I got a call from my father saying, "If you don't come home, you can't talk to your siblings anymore."

I had to make that choice of me over anyone else. I felt really guilty and selfish for choosing myself over my brother, but even now, if I had to do it again, I would have to choose me. He may not have been okay. He was alive. I'm not okay. But, I'm alive. That's how I'm living every single day right now. I'm not okay, but I'm alive, and that has to be enough. I didn't even have that strength until my father called me and offered me money to keep my mouth shut. He told me he was offering it to me to never talk about it. I don't even know how much I was molested and raped.

I remember a doctor's appointment. He was concerned about how fast I was developing. I think he was worried that I was pregnant. I remember being very very young when I started my period. I was very young, probably eight. It's kind of a mystery—one that will remain that way until I can get my father to admit everything he has done to me.

My self-esteem was zero. He totally destroyed me and any hope I had for finding love and for having a future more than what he painted—which was never leaving home because no one would ever want me.

After I got that phone call from him where he offered to pay me off if i agreed to never talk about the sexual assault, it started to make sense. It's like something just clicked in. It was really upsetting. I wanted to fucking shave my head, and so I did. At that moment, it was because of a lot of reasons, but primarily it was because my dad used to threaten me that if I would get a bad grade he would shave my head. I would have to go to school bald. Of course, as a kid that's like the worst thing you could possibly imagine because I would be ridiculed and I didn't want that. I wanted friends, but it didn't matter because I didn't really have any. I decided to shave my head. I didn't give a fuck what anybody thought about me. I just felt like I'm going to live in my truth and I know that my heart is pure and my soul is pure and that is good enough and if anybody has shit to say to me, they can surely try, but I don't need to respond. I feel strong in my convictions, but I feel weak at the same time because of my environment.

A Positive Response

On 3/21/2022 I called the cops on myself because Dylan thought I wasn't being a good mom. I ended up checking into a mental facility for 2 weeks as a result. Honestly, it was scary and it was the hardest thing I ever did, but at the time I thought it had to be done. Now, honestly coming back from it is harder than being there. Having to be a mom immediately, jump back into it and try to also take care of myself is proving to feel impossible, and I have to lean on Dylan for a lot, because I'm somebody who can't stand being touched and can't stand screaming and yelling. Having two babies under three years old, was not a wise decision, but obviously, I love them, and I would change it. That doesn't mean that I don't struggle because of what I've been through.

What's most important is that you know, you are not alone that there will always be somebody in your corner that loves you and cares about you and wants the very best for you. There is someone that will carry the burdens for you, because she is strong enough to do that. I've carried my own burden for years and many, many other people's because that's who I am. I'm a healer and my mother used to tell me that I am attracted to broken people. I am so attracted to broken because of how deeply, deeply, deeply broken I am. I am a plate on a shelf that has been knocked over and shattered all over the floor and then haphazardly put back together over the years. So if anybody is fucked up, it's me, and you should not be ashamed or afraid of me or your own truth of anything because I'm living proof that you can literally be in psychosis live on Facebook or have a spiritual awakening on Facebook and still have such a positive response.

Mending with Gold

In the hospital, you would wake up at 6:00 am, breakfast at 7:00am, meds at 8:00 am and then they would just have groups throughout the day until meds at 8:00 pm. I loved the structure honestly and I loved having three square meals a day. I was being taken care of and doing things I love. Writing, singing, talking with people who understand, etc. No phones, no computers, just people.

For example, they had one group on coping mechanisms and what your triggers look like, and how your body looks when you're triggered. I really, really remember this one, because it just stood out to me. I have a lot of triggers, so I wrote them all down. I thought about them and then I put honestly how I react, like my chest gets tight, I feel angry, I'm going to scream, my eyes start to water. When we were talking about it, they were discussing ways to cope, and they suggested singing. I remembered how much I used to love singing and so each day, I would just sing in my room and people would walk by my door, and they would just tell me how amazing of a singer I am and that would just blow me away.

Honestly, what healed me the most was having these people look at this bald headed, no eyebrows woman and still want to be her friend, still want to get to know her, still think she's valuable as a person. Despite all of the things that society has told us is beautiful—I was at my lowest mentally and physically and I didn't look like your typical beautiful girl, I looked like a little baby—and no one batted an eyelash. These groups, they were amazing.

Being in the groups taught me what I needed to learn. Healing things that I needed to hear and really accept.

1. Who I am is okay.

2. I can listen and empathize.

3. Being vulnerable is okay.

Who I am is okay, and even though I just said you shouldn't care about other people's opinions, I don't, but when they have these nice things to say to me, of course, it's going to make me feel special and loved.

On my Facebook page, I got to talk to somebody on a real level about real shit that weren't my problems, they were someone else's problems that I could listen to and I could say, I've been through that too, I know what you mean or I haven't been through that but I can understand why you decided to rob a bank or whatever. I'm not going to judge anyone, because I know how bad it feels to be judged.

Once you decide to finally step over that line of 'this is what I want the world to see and what I don't', once you just erase that line and let the world see who you are, you have so much power, because nothing is going to be able to tear you down. Nobody is going to be able to say anything to me that I haven't heard before. I just won't even allow it to hurt my feelings. It's like it's not even hitting me. It's like you know that saying "I'm rubber, you're glue. Anything you say to me bounces off me and sticks to you." That's how I feel now.

I'll play Call of Duty and I can have people trash talk me and it doesn't matter. I'll go on online here and I'll have people laugh at the fact that I'm charging a certain amount for my service and that doesn't bother me. I just say, "Okay, have a good day." That's the power of vulnerability. You don't have to have the weight of other people's opinions on your shoulders. You're free from all that bullshit and all you need to do is answer to yourself and make yourself proud and that's it.

What kept me from being free when I left home was my brother. That always kind of tied me to my parents, even though I hated them, I would go and visit them so that I could see my brother. I think I visited them maybe three times since I moved out just to see Josh. We would have the best time and he would be so happy and it would just make my heart so happy. I would have kept going—I mean hell, I was still talking to my parents up until not too long ago, because I had a hope that they would change, I had a hope that I was wrong, I had a hope that they might be grandparents to my children and they were pretty encouraging of that hope, even though it was all fucking lies—I enjoyed my time with my brother so much.

I will forever love my brother. I've never loved anyone more than I've loved my brother—except my own children—and to know that he has been hurt and possibly by my dad as well just kills me. I feel like I could have prevented it but I know I couldn't have. If he was going to do it, he was going to do it, whether or not I was around to stop it and I realize that now. That would have made me free back then, but I kept coming back home for him.

It's just easier to believe that there is still goodness, and light and love in the world than to believe how dark it really was. My brain couldn't even comprehend that kind of abuse, and I think that's why I disassociated from it.

I look at my own children now, and to think that a father or a mother could just sit idly by while molestation and physical abuse and emotional abuse are happening... I couldn't imagine it.

I think I had to separate myself at a young age from what was happening. I had to go somewhere else in my mind and that's why some of these memories are like a dream. I just wasn't connected to it at all. I kept lying to myself saying, "Oh they're going to help me with a job" or "They can help me with the money to move into this apartment." That made them good people or was a sign of redemption for them somehow. I kept hoping that was true because I think everyone at the end of the day, wants their parents to love them and I wanted to believe that my parents did love me. They just didn't.

I am here to offer a service, one that would allow you to completely come clean and live a truthful happy life. The demons we hide will eventually take over the soul, and I would like to vanquish and carry those demons for you because I am strong enough to

endure them.

41

Worth So Much

Listen. You are so beautiful. You are worth so much more than you can even imagine. I want you to just go to Disney world and not worry about anything besides having the time of your life. You don't want to waste that opportunity and you don't want to be trapped in a relationship for five years, with someone who doesn't even love you but who feels like they have to take care of you, because they stole your virginity.

Focus on your work and on Disney and just being happy. Go to the parks to make friends with everyone that you can. Fall in love, but don't fall for the wrong kind of guy. You have to fall for the guy that you know exists because you've watched it in movies. Yes, maybe not to that level they don't exist but fuck, they exist more than what you think!

You are worth so much more than a man that mistreats you and wants you to do his laundry and to fucking feed him or have sex with him.

So now, I want to ask you. Are you okay? How are you coping with everything that's been thrown at you? While it might seem like you are alone in this world, there are a lot of services out there that can help you.

Professional help is available, but if that's too intimidating, there's friends that you might be able to open up to. There's teachers that you might be able to open up to. Everybody that you think is closed off from hearing your story might not be closed off to hearing your story. I think that you should tell your story and scream it as loud as you can from the rooftops!

I'm beautiful inside and now I love me even when I'm mad and when I'm not myself, even when I step out of the shower I'm completely naked and have all of my scars and everything exposed, I'm beautiful. With no hair, with no eyebrows, with nothing... my soul is beautiful.

I hope that my soul has impacted you in some way. In calls that I have had with clients, the biggest thing I realized is that people don't expect me to be so non-judgmental and so open with my feelings with them. The major breakthrough that they have is just being able to trust that I'm going to carry their secrets or carry their conversations with me as close to my heart as I can, so that way they can be free of it.

One woman, whom I recently checked in on, told me that she took my advice, and now she is no longer dating a loser, she is moving out of state for a new job—one that fits her heart so well—and she has done nothing but move onward and upward.

The biggest and best advice I can give you:

1. Do one thing that really fucking scares you.

Whether it's singing karaoke in front of a bunch of people or shaving your head bald or going a day without makeup or something along those lines, do one thing that really fucking terrifies you publicly, and do it as publicly as you can.

2. Next, protect your virginity. [Make sure you are completely ready... sex should be a

vulnerable act out of love only pure and true love.]

3. Protect your heart. [Don't fall for the first kindness. Make them earn your heart do not give it freely away for anything. Especially if they are not reciprocating.

You Are Gold

Everything that you're afraid of in life, just fucking throw it away because none of it matters. You're never going to be happy, unless you live in your truth, unless you bare your soul to everyone around you. That's important. If they don't know the real you, then they love a lie. That's what I had to tell Dylan. He didn't even give me the choice to really love him. He gave me the choice to love the facade that he created for me.

So don't do that shit. Don't be fake, be genuine. Be authentic, be real and raw, and don't be scared of other people's opinions, because the right people will stay in your corner and the wrong ones will fucking flush themselves out.

While you're definitely beautiful on the outside, people will take advantage of that beauty and people will want that beauty around them, but they won't know what to do with it. Keep that guard up until you find somebody who's worthy of your heart.

The moment we met, the moment you started reading this book, I fell in love with your soul. I care about you. I would like to offer my contact information below so that you can reach me whenever you need to, and so that you know that in this life, you're never truly alone.

Keep yourself safe and enjoy Disney World and your dreams. Go chase your dreams and do not be scared to fail. Even if it's hard, cut your family out completely if that's the boundary you need to set.

We are the world, we have the power to make a change, and we have to start with ourselves. Look at the woman in the mirror. We have to be completely honest with who we are, completely honest with how we failed and how it felt. We are the world and we have the power to fix the world.

I knew this in my mind. Now I know it in the depth of my soul.

I had a religious experience in 2017, but I had fallen away and then…

April 20th 2022

I was listening to a minister, and he just kept saying "I know you are searching for that missing piece"

Yes! I thought that is me!

And then he did the prayer of salvation and I fell to pieces

"and Jesus - scooping the precious gem out of the shit, shining her, polishing her, whispering in her ear <I LOVE YOU> all the pieces that were missing - all that she thought was shattered beyond repair were made better than mended with gold. All of the perfect her she always was fell into place...she had the one and only thing that she ever needed - JESUS"

(This is a quote from Steve Kidd, he was online with me, showing me God's love and sharing worship songs with me. And this quote was his response to this salvation/transformation experience I had)

And Now I am here to help you!

Go to:

https://www.facebook.com/Magikinthemundane

I look forward to talking with you!